Awesome Dinosaurs
MEAT EATERS

Michael Benton

COPPER BEECH BOOKS
Brookfield, Connecticut

© Aladdin Books Ltd 2001

Produced by:
Aladdin Books Ltd
28 Percy Street
London W1P 0LD

ISBN 0–7613–2158–6

*First published in the United
States in 2001 by:*
Copper Beech Books,
an imprint of
The Millbrook Press
2 Old New Milford Road
Brookfield,
Connecticut 06804

Editor:
Kathy Gemmell

Designer:
Flick, Book Design & Graphics

Illustrators:
James Field, Ross Watton—SGA
Additional illustrations:
Sarah Smith—SGA
Cartoons: Jo Moore

Certain illustrations have
appeared in earlier
books created by
Aladdin Books.

Cataloging-in-Publication data is
on file at the Library of Congress.

Contents

Introduction

Find out for yourself all about the fearsome meat-eating dinosaurs that roamed Earth millions and millions of years ago.

Dinosaurs were among the most successful animals of all time. They lived on Earth for many, many years. Scientists called paleontologists are constantly unearthing amazing information and making exciting new discoveries about meat eaters and the dinosaurs that lived with them. They study their remains, called fossils, which have been preserved in ancient rocks.

Spot and count!

Q: Why watch out for these boxes?

A: They give answers to the meat eater questions you always wanted to ask.

zoom in on...

Dinosaur bits

Look out for these boxes to take a closer look at meat eater features.

Awesome facts

Watch out for these diamonds to learn more about the truly weird and wonderful facts about meat eaters and their world.

MESOZOIC ERA: 250–65 MILLION YEARS AGO (MYA)
The Mesozoic era, when the dinosaurs lived, is split into three periods.

Triassic period: 250–205 mya
Meat eaters appeared halfway through this time.

Jurassic period: 205–145 mya
Age of giant dinosaurs and first birds.

Cretaceous period: 145–65 mya
A time of success for meat eaters. Their last phase.

Fish, amphibians, and early reptiles appeared before the Mesozoic era.

250 mya

205 mya

145 mya

65 mya

Today

Age of the dinosaurs

The dinosaurs lived between 230 and 65 million years ago (mya). This is a very long time, and it was a very long time ago. It's hard enough to imagine hundreds of years ago, let alone millions. Scientists know when dinosaurs lived because they can date the rocks in which their fossils are found. They do this by studying the radioactivity of the rocks, then classing them on a scale called the geological time scale. This is split into sections called eras.

4

At the start of the age of the dinosaurs, the continents were all joined together as one great supercontinent called Pangaea. Over millions of years, the Atlantic Ocean opened up and Pangaea split apart. The continents drifted (moved slowly) to their present positions. They are still moving a few inches each year.

Today

50 mya

100 mya

Pangaea

200 mya

Continental drift

Q: How did a meat-eating dinosaur become a fossil?

A: Small meat-eating animals ate the flesh from the dead dinosaur's bones. Some bones rotted. Others were buried under layers of sand or mud. These turned into fossils over time, as tiny spaces in the bones filled with rock. Millions of years later, the fossilized bones are uncovered by water or wind action. Paleontologists dig the fossilized bones out of the rock and clean them, making sure they don't fall apart. They make maps and take photographs at the dig site so that they can tell later exactly where everything was found.

Big meat eaters
like *T. rex* ate
the larger
plant eaters.
T. rex probably
wasn't very fast
or very bright.
It didn't need to
be. It was so big,
it could attack
almost any
other dinosaur.

Tyrannosaurus rex

Troodon

T. rex used its massive
teeth to tear strips
from its prey's flesh.

Big and small

The meat eaters were part of the dinosaur group called the theropods. They ranged from small, turkey-sized dinosaurs to the awesome *Tyrannosaurus rex.* Theropods of different sizes ate prey of different sizes. This meant that several species could live side by side.

Ornithomimus

In the Late Cretaceous of Canada, smaller meat eaters lived alongside the huge *T. rex.* *Troodon* hunted lizards, mammals, and even insects. It relied on speed and intelligence. *Ornithomimus* ate small plant-eating dinosaurs and the young of larger ones.

What is
T. rex
eating?

7

What makes a meat eater?

All meat eaters had sharp claws.
They also had sharp, curved teeth
pointing backward that pushed any
struggling prey farther into the gaping
jaws. One of the most fearsome
meat eaters was *Deinonychus*.

Deinonychus

Q: How did *Deinonychus* use
its toe claw?

A: It had one huge claw on each
foot, on the second toe. When
running, it held the
claw off the ground
so it would not
become blunt.
But when it
attacked, it raised
its foot and slashed
downward with the
claw, as shown here.

8

Deinonychus was only as tall as a ten-year-old child, so it had to work in packs to bring down large prey like this *Tenontosaurus*.

Tenontosaurus

zoom in on...

Balancing

Two-legged dinosaurs, like *Deinonychus* and the other meat eaters, were like seesaws, balanced over their back legs. The front of the body had to weigh the same as the tail, or the dinosaur would fall on its nose. It had to hold its backbone flat when it ran and flick its massive tail around to keep its balance.

Awesome facts

Most dinosaurs were pretty stupid, but *Deinonychus* had a big brain. It needed it, in order to balance, see well, and be able to communicate with the rest of the pack.

Smash and grab

One of the first meat-eating dinosaurs was *Herrerasaurus*, from the Late Triassic of Argentina, 230 million years ago. Medium-sized and good at hunting, *Herrerasaurus* ate mammal-like reptiles called cynodonts, which lived in burrows.

Herrerasaurus

Herrerasaurus had the advantage in a sudden attack. It could creep up silently, dart its head into a cynodont burrow, and race off with a cub before the parent could do anything.

Q: How did dinosaur jaws open so wide?

A: Most meat eaters had very narrow skulls. There wasn't much in there except teeth and jaw muscles— the brain was pretty tiny. But when a meat eater opened its jaws, its whole mouth stretched sideways to take a bigger bite.

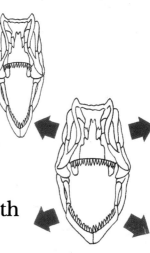

The ancestors of mammals belonged to the same mammal-like reptile group as cynodonts. Some cynodonts probably had hair and were warm-blooded. They could hunt at night, unlike the cold-blooded early dinosaurs.

Meat eaters had powerful hands. Early ones, like *Herrerasaurus*, had four or five muscular fingers, each with a long, sharp claw. Most later meat eaters had only three fingers, and some, like *T. rex*, had only two.

Cynodont

zoom in on...

Predator numbers

Meat eaters were much rarer than plant eaters. This is because there must always be far fewer predators than prey animals, like lions and antelope today.

11

Hunt to the death

Fossilized footprints show that meat-eating dinosaurs walked and swam in lakes. The eighteen-foot-long *Ceratosaurus* was the terror of North America 150 million years ago. But it took more than one to bring down *Apatosaurus*, a huge but slow-moving plant eater.

Awesome factS

Ceratosaurus had horns on its head, in front of the eyes. These made it look more frightening and may have been used for fighting.

Ceratosaurus

 Q: Why did meat eater skulls have so many holes?

A: Holes are lighter than bones, and a light skull can move faster. So a meat eater had thin bones with very big holes between them for its ears, eyes, nostrils, and jaw muscles.

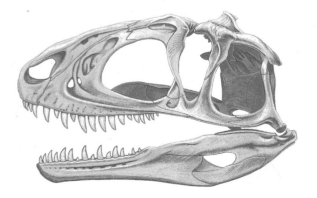

Small and medium-sized meat eaters like *Ceratosaurus* could run fast. They moved at twelve to eighteen miles per hour, which is about the fastest you could sprint over a short distance. Bigger meat eaters like *Albertosaurus* may not have been able to move as fast because they were so much heavier.

Albertosaurus

Apatosaurus

Pack hunting was a risky business. Although *Apatosaurus* did not have powerful teeth or sharp claws, it could whack out with its powerful tail and stun a predator. But if the *Ceratosaurus* kept biting into its flesh, the *Apatosaurus* would eventually become weak and die.

13

What's in a name?

Dinosaur means "terrible lizard." Although we now know that they were not lizards, dinosaur names often tell us something about them. Named in 1884, savage meat eater *Ceratosaurus* means "horned lizard," referring to the horns on its face.

Megalosaurus "big lizard"

Dilophosaurus "two-ridged lizard"

The fierce meat eater *Yangchuanosaurus*, from an area of China called Yangchuan, attacks a Chinese plant eater.

Yangchuanosaurus "Yangchuan lizard"

Archaeopteryx "ancient wing"

Q: Who gives dinosaurs their names?

A: Dinosaurs are named by their discoverers. About twenty new species are still being named every year. If you find a new dinosaur skeleton, which has never been named, you can make up a name and publish it!

Megalosaurus, named in 1824, means "big lizard." This drawing shows what scientists then thought it looked like.

Sir Richard Owen made up the word "dinosaur" in 1842.

Othniel Marsh (left) and Edward Cope (right) named more dinosaurs than anyone else between 1870 and 1900, including *Ceratosaurus, Allosaurus,* and *Stegosaurus.*

Ceratosaurus
"horned lizard"

zoom in on...

Skull horns

Allosaurus, like most meat eaters, had knobs and lumps on its skull. What were they for? Maybe they just made its face look more scary. When male dinosaurs squared up to each other, *Allosaurus*, with its loud growl and its bumps, would usually have been the winner.

Allosaurus

How many flies can you count?

All over the world

Meat eaters lived all over the world. *Allosaurus*, for example, is best known from the Late Jurassic of North America, 150 million years ago, but remains have also been found in Tanzania in Africa and possibly even in Australia.

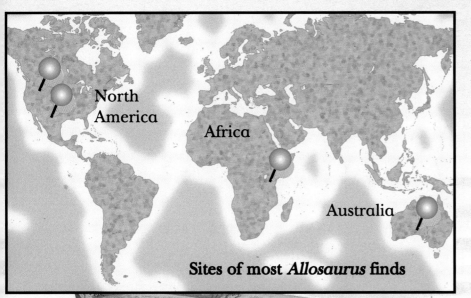

North America

Africa

Australia

Sites of most *Allosaurus* finds

The worldwide spread of *Allosaurus* is not surprising when you remember that the continents were joined together as the supercontinent Pangaea in the Jurassic (see page 5). *Allosaurus* could have wandered from one end of the world to the other.

Awesome facts

The Australian *Allosaurus* find is not confirmed. It is in Early Cretaceous rocks, 50 million years younger than the other finds, and is only of part of a leg.

Tiny and terrible

Some meat eaters were so tiny that a big plant-eating dinosaur like *Apatosaurus* would not even see them. But these midgets were pretty scary if you were a ratlike mammal or a lizard. Small size went with intelligence and speed.

Compsognathus lived in what is now Germany, and was the smallest dinosaur— a mere twenty-three inches long from its snout to the tip of its tail. An amazing fossil of this tiny hunter (right) even shows its last meal—a complete skeleton of the lizard *Bavarisaurus*, inside its rib cage.

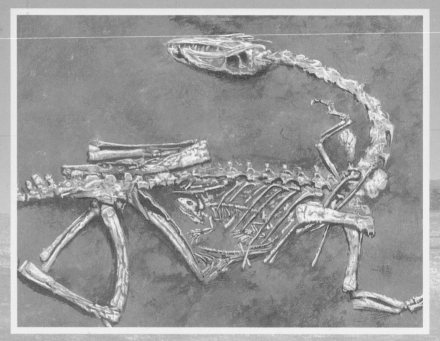

Awesome facts
When *Compsognathus* was found in 1861, it was not recognized as a dinosaur because it was thought to be too small.

A small flock of *Compsognathus* are scattered (right) by a giant plant eater. These little dinosaurs could move fast. They may even have had a fine covering of feathers over their bodies. They fed on lizards, frogs, and dragonflies.

Q: Were some dinosaurs really as small as chickens?

A: If the fully adult *Compsognathus* was only twenty-three inches long, its babies must have been tiny. Scientists know about quite a number of dinosaur young, and many of them were the size of a chicken, or even smaller.

Compsognathus

19

Feathers are made from keratin, the same horny protein that makes up your nails and your hair. Feathers are not often preserved as fossils because they normally rot before the carcass is buried. However, in some cases, if the feather is buried quickly, it can survive as a fossil.

Sinosauropteryx

Feathered find

Until the 1990s, feathered dinosaurs were only a wild theory. Then some startling finds in China proved that many small meat eaters had them. *Sinosauropteryx* is one of the newly discovered Chinese feathered dinosaurs, and is thought to be a relative of *Compsognathus*.

Compsognathus and *Archaeopteryx,* the first bird, were found in the same rocks in southern Germany. Both were named in 1861. Paleontologists soon noticed that their skeletons were very similar, and they suggested that dinosaurs had given rise to birds. This has been debated hotly for years, but it now seems clear that birds really are living theropod dinosaurs.

Archaeopteryx

Compsognathus

zoom in on...

Wings

A wing is just a fairly long arm that has feathers on it. *Deinonychus* had long arms with strong hands, probably covered with short feathers. It is not hard to see how this could have evolved into a flying wing if the feathers grew longer.

Deinonychus

Fishing claws

Most meat eaters ate other dinosaurs or smaller land animals. One group, the spinosaurids, had crocodile-shaped skulls and may have been fish eaters. Perhaps they used their strong hands to swipe fish out of the water, just as bears do today.

Awesome facts

The spinosaurid *Baryonyx* from southern England was found by accident in 1983 by William Walker as he walked through his local brickyard.

Baryonyx

Q: Why did spinosaurids have crocodile skulls?

A: The long, low snout and numerous teeth of the spinosaurids must have been ideal for holding struggling fish. Stronger jaws are needed only for larger prey. Spinosaurids looked far more like modern crocodiles than like other meat eaters.

Crocodile

22

Some spinosaurids had long spines on their vertebrae (backbone). These may have had a thin covering of skin—a kind of sail—running along them. Perhaps this was used to control body temperature—to take in heat when the body was cold and to give it off when the body was overheated.

The spinosaurid *Baryonyx*, from the Early Cretaceous of southern England, crouched silently beside a river and swiped out fish with its long-clawed hand.

Oviraptor means "egg thief." It was named in 1924, and has had a bad reputation ever since. Paleontologists then thought that this toothless theropod fed on eggs. But the reason it was found close to nests containing eggs was that it was a good parent, caring for its own young!

Oviraptor

How many eggs can you count?

zoom in on...

Dinosaur eggs

Scientists dissect dinosaur eggs, and sometimes they find tiny bones inside. This tiny embryo lay curled up inside the eggshell—it must have died before it could hatch.

Oviraptor embryo

24

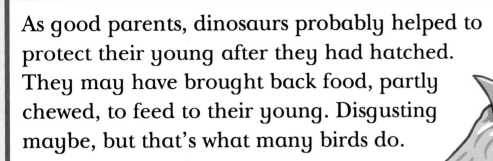

As good parents, dinosaurs probably helped to protect their young after they had hatched. They may have brought back food, partly chewed, to feed to their young. Disgusting maybe, but that's what many birds do.

Nesting

An astonishing find in 1995 in Mongolia showed that some meat eaters sat on their eggs, just like modern birds do, to protect them and keep them warm (or cool). Most modern reptiles lay their eggs then leave them.

Q: How big was a *T. rex* tooth?

A: *T. rex* had teeth the size of steak knives. The tooth had two halves. The upper crown, which did the cutting, was the size of a banana. The root, hidden in the jawbone, was just as big.

T. rex—terrifying hunter or humble scavenger? Some paleontologists think that *T. rex* was so massive that it could not have moved fast. It might have lumbered about slowly, looking for rotting carcasses that had been killed by smaller, swifter meat eaters.

Sizing up

The meat-eating dinosaur *Tyrannosaurus rex*, from the Late Cretaceous of North America, was a monster. At thirty-nine feet long and weighing up to nearly nine tons, *T. rex* was truly awesome: It could swallow you in one gulp. But was it the biggest?

T. rex footprint

Other huge dinosaurs, such as *Carcharodontosaurus* from North Africa and *Giganotosaurus* from Argentina, may have been longer than *T. rex*, but they were not as heavy.

Tyrannosaurus rex

zoom in on...

Poop!

In 1998, Canadian scientists found a giant dinosaur poop, about three feet long, containing dinosaur bones. Whodunnit? *T. rex*, most probably.

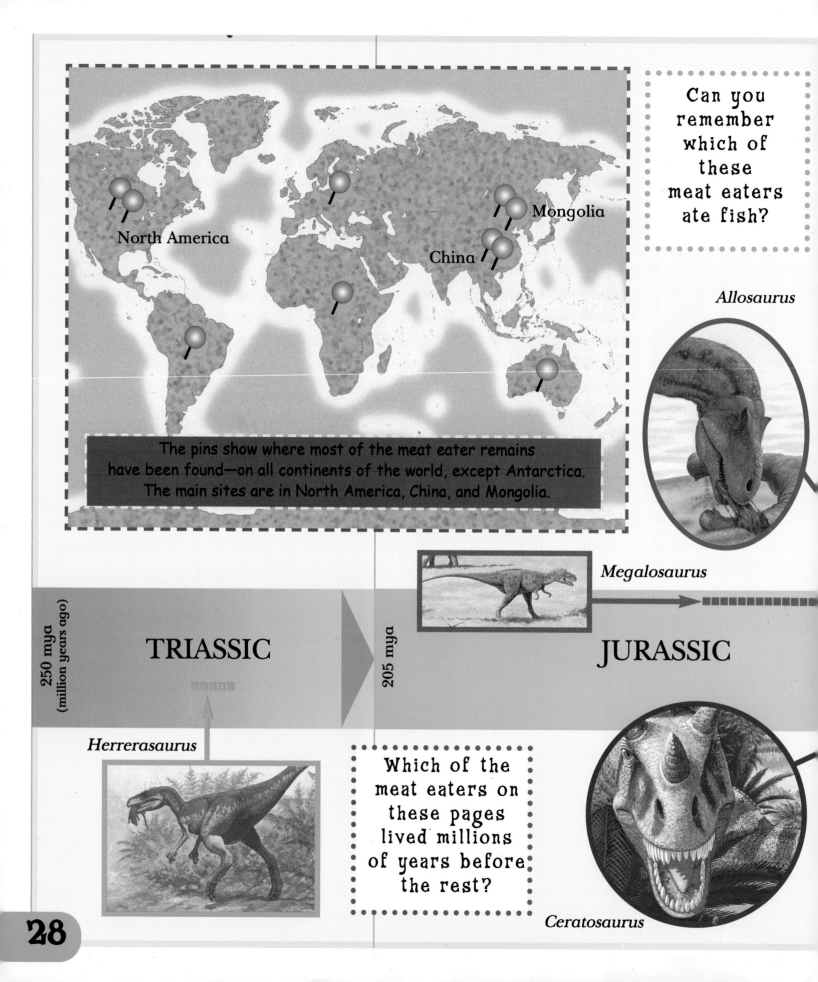

North America

Mongolia

China

The pins show where most of the meat eater remains have been found—on all continents of the world, except Antarctica. The main sites are in North America, China, and Mongolia.

Can you remember which of these meat eaters ate fish?

Allosaurus

Megalosaurus

250 mya (million years ago)

TRIASSIC

205 mya

JURASSIC

Herrerasaurus

Which of the meat eaters on these pages lived millions of years before the rest?

Ceratosaurus

28

Meat eaters' world

From the tiny *Compsognathus* to the awesome *T. rex*, theropods were the terrors of the Mesozoic era. They are known from all corners of the world and existed for 165 million years.

T. rex

Sinosauropteryx

Albertosaurus

Baryonyx

Oviraptor

CRETACEOUS

145 mya

65 mya

Compsognathus

Deinonychus

Ornithomimus

Troodon

Dinosaur groups

There were five main groups of dinosaur: the meat eaters (theropods); the big, long-necked plant eaters, called sauropodomorphs; the armored plant eaters, called thyreophorans; the horned dinosaurs, called marginocephalians; and the two-legged plant eaters, called ornithopods.

Tyrannosaurus rex

Diplodocus

Sauropelta

Einosaurus

Corythosaurus

All dinosaurs are classed into one of two subgroups, the Saurischia and the Ornithischia, according to the arrangement of their three hip bones. The Saurischia, or "lizard hips," had the three hip bones all pointing in different directions. The Ornithischia, or "bird hips," had both of the lower hip bones running backward.

Hypsilophodon (Ornithischia)

Carnotaurus (Saurischia)

Glossary

Amphibian

A backboned animal that lives both in water and on land, such as a frog.

Cold-blooded

A cold-blooded animal needs to take its body heat from outside sources, like the sun.

Continental drift

The movement of the continents over time.

Cretaceous

The geological period that lasted from 145 to 65 million years ago.

Cynodont

A mammal-like reptile similar to the very first mammals.

Fossil

The remains of any ancient plant or animal, usually preserved in rock.

Geological

To do with the study of rocks.

Jurassic

The geological period that lasted from 205 to 145 million years ago.

Mammal

A backboned animal with hair which feeds its young on milk, like a cat or a human.

Mesozoic

The geological era that lasted from 250 to 65 million years ago. Also called the "age of dinosaurs."

Paleontologist

A person who studies fossils.

Predator

A meat eater—an animal that hunts other animals for food.

Radioactivity

"Rays" of chemical energy that are given off at fixed rates. Measuring radioactive elements in ancient rocks allows geologists to calculate the age of the rocks.

Reptile

A backboned animal with scales, such as a dinosaur or a lizard. Most reptiles lay eggs and live on land.

Scavenger

A meat eater that feeds off animals that have died or have been killed by others.

Species

One particular kind of plant or animal, such as *Tyrannosaurus rex*, the panda, or human beings.

Theropod

A meat-eating dinosaur.

Triassic

The geological period that lasted from 250 to 205 million years ago.

Vertebra (plural **Vertebrae**)

Together, the vertebrae make up the backbone. Each vertebra is like a cotton spool with bits sticking out for the ribs and muscles.

Warm-blooded

A warm-blooded animal, such as a mammal or a bird, creates heat inside its body from the food it eats.

Index